THE featured Violinist

FREE piano accompaniments and
audio backing tracks available online.
Visit: www.featuredseries.com
Registration is free and easy.
Your registration code is: MR340

Boston Music Company
part of The Music Sales Group
New York/Los Angeles/Nashville/London/Berlin/Copenhagen/Madrid/Paris/Sydney/Tokyo

Published by
Boston Music Company

Exclusive Distributors:
Music Sales Corporation
257 Park Avenue South, New York, NY 10010 USA

Music Sales Limited
14-15 Berners Street, London W1T 3LJ England

Music Sales Pty. Limited
120 Rothschild Street, Rosebery, Sydney, NSW 2018, Australia

Order No. BMC-11968
ISBN 0-8256-3479-2

This book © Copyright 2006 Boston Music Company,
A division of Music Sales Corporation, New York

Translated & edited by Rebecca Taylor.

Printed in the United States of America by
Vicks Lithograph and Printing Corporation

Your Guarantee of Quality:
As publishers, we strive to produce every book
to the highest commercial standards.

The book has been carefully designed to minimize awkward page turns
and to make playing from it a real pleasure. Particular care has been given
to specifying acid-free, neutral-sized paper made from pulps
which have not been elemental chlorine bleached.

This pulp is from farmed sustainable forests and
was produced with special regard for the environment.

Throughout, the printing and binding have been planned
to ensure a sturdy, attractive publication which should give
years of enjoyment.

If your copy fails to meet our high standards, please inform us
and we will gladly replace it.

www.musicsales.com

Air On The G String

Music by Johann Sebastian Bach

Hungarian Dance No.4

Music by Johannes Brahms

Orientale

Music by César Cui

Humoresque

Music by Antonín Dvořák

Pizzicato
(from 'Sylvia')
Music by Léo Delibes

Slavonic Dance No.10

Music by Antonín Dvořák

Salut D'Amour

Music by Edvard Elgar

Liebestraum

Music by Franz Liszt

Méditation
(from 'Thais')

Music by Jules Massenet

Norwegian Dance

Music by Edvard Grieg

Violin Concerto
(Second Movement: Andante)

Music by Felix Mendelssohn

Spring Song

Music by Felix Mendelssohn

Cavatina

Music by Joachim Raff

Melody In F

Music by Anton Rubinstein

Serenade

Music by Franz Schubert

Träumerei

Music by Robert Schumann

Chant Sans Paroles

Music by Pyotr Ilyich Tchaikovsky

CD Track Listing

1. **Air On The G String**
    (Bach)
2. **Hungarian Dance No.4**
    (Brahms)
3. **Orientale**
    (Cui)
4. **Humoresque**
    (Dvořàk)
5. **Pizzicato (from 'Sylvia')**
    (Delibes)
6. **Slavonic Dance No.10**
    (Dvořàk)
7. **Salut D'Amour**
    (Elgar)
8. **Liebestraum**
    (Liszt)
9. **Méditation (from 'Thais')**
    (Massenet)

10. **Norwegian Dance**
    (Grieg)
11. **Violin Concerto (Second Movement: Andante)**
    (Mendelssohn)
12. **Spring Song**
    (Mendelssohn)
13. **Cavatina**
    (Raff)
14. **Melody In F**
    (Rubinstein)
15. **Serenade**
    (Schubert)
16. **Träumerei**
    (Schumann)
17. **Chant Sans Paroles**
    (Tchaikovsky)